Footnotes on a landscape – 6

give me your
painting hand

W. S. GRAHAM
& Cornwall

David Whittaker

wavestone
press

In memory of Michael & Margaret Snow
'I am trying to be better'

Give Me Your Painting Hand: W. S. Graham & Cornwall

ISBN: 978-09545194-8-3

Wavestone Press, 6 Rochester Place, Charlbury, Oxon OX7 3SF
Phone: 01608-811435; email: wavestone@btinternet.com
Web: www.wavestonepress.co.uk

I was privileged to have been a friend over many years to Michael and Margaret Snow. Their selfless dedication to promoting the legacy of WSG was exemplary, as was their generosity in sharing this knowledge with anyone who showed a genuine interest. An early draft of this essay was met with an enthusiastic 'bravo' that gave me the confidence to aim for something more ambitious. I can only hope their reposing Shades may be alerted to at least a smile and a gentle nod of approval to the final product. A very special thanks to Justin Snow for permitting the use of Michael's superb photographs.

Speaking of Shades: I also offer a bow of gratitude to those now resident in the Elysian Fields (I hope you are keeping well): Wilhelmina Barns-Graham, Graham Binns, Jeremy Le Grice, Roger Slack, Nancy Wynne-Jones, Monica Wynter. The quality time they kindly offered me in conversations has no doubt filtered into the text in one way or another.

Among the living, as I write, I must thank: Janet Axten, Christopher Barker, Michael Bird, Sophie Bowness, Robert Brennan, Ronnie Duncan, Sally Fear, Gail Featherston, Matthew Francis, Rose Hilton, Andrew Lanyon, Lawrence Lawry, Barry Lopez, Valerie Lowndes, Mayotte Magnus, Roz Mudalier, Jane O'Malley, Jonathan Riley, Michael Schmidt, Tony Shiels, Sylvia Thompson, Billy Wynter.

With profound gratitude to the following subscribers, your benevolent contributions helped ease some of the anxieties of production: Ronnie Duncan, Paul Francis, Rose Hilton, Joy & Ray Kell, Neville Shack, Luís & Mary de Sousa, Peter Strong, plus those benefactors who chose anonymity over being immortalised in the Wavestone Hall of Fame!

My wife Penny and daughter Alice acted as good lighthouse beacons guiding me clear of the rocks in choppy waters. It was with relief I frequently collapsed into their 'boatfilled arms'!

Thanks again to Keith Rigley: it's always a great joy to hear the tune in my head become manifest on his Stradivarius (in a manner of speaking)!

Main text set in Brioso; elsewhere a mix of Poetica & Zapfino
Book design & production: David Whittaker & Keith Rigley
Printed by Henry Ling Ltd, Dorchester, Dorset

Contents

WSG with Anthony Benjamin

Give Me Your Painting Hand

On November 19, 1918 – eight days after the world declared an armistice on the greatest period of human hostilities known in recorded history – William Sydney Graham unleashed the sound of his lungs for his first primitive act of communication and dependence with an unidentified personage 'out there'. He would persevere heroically in this temper, albeit in slightly more hushed and intricate tones, until his death 67 years later in 1986.

Since then, with the publication of his sparkling correspondence followed by a new collected edition of his poetry, Graham is now perceived to be one of the most original and challenging writers of the latter half of the twentieth century. His work exemplifies the struggle of a single-minded poet with the ambiguities inherent in the raw material of words as a dependable means of linguistic transmission. Graham was acutely aware of the absurd paradox that the poem he constructed in solipsistic isolation was then expected to go forth and make some meaningful, social impact on a community of readers or listeners. But there was a price to pay for such total commitment. He endured a lifetime of exceptional financial hardship accompanied by critical neglect, he also remained troubled by a self-exile's sense of culpability, in his case at forsaking his industrial working class heritage in Scotland by moving to the opposite end of the British Isles.

Graham was born at 1 Hope Street, Greenock, then a prosperous Clydeside town whose wealth was based on its docks, shipyards and sugar refineries. This busy maritime location infused the young Graham's imagination with notions of the sea, sailing and travel that lasted throughout his life. His mother, Margaret (née McDermid), who he claimed was from Galway, ran a small general shop, while his father, Alexander, was a journeyman engineer.

The local schooling failed to engage Graham's interest in any way. Known to his friends as Sydney, he preferred wandering alone over the hills and far away. At fourteen he left school and was apprenticed as a draughtsman to a Glasgow engineering firm. While singing in the Trinity Church choir there was a fleeting opportunity to develop an unexpected career when the choirmaster offered to have Graham's fine tenor voice professionally trained, but the offer was declined. Nevertheless, wherever he was and whatever the circumstances he had an enduring love of breaking into song.

In 1938 Graham had a remarkable stroke of luck when he was awarded a bursary to spend an academic year at Newbattle Abbey College for mature students. He attended classes on economics, early Scottish literature, English literature – including Anglo-Saxon poetry, Coleridge, Wordsworth, Yeats, Synge, Joyce, Eliot and Pound – as well as philosophy. Graham was very taken by the fragmentary musings of the pre-Socratics, notably Heraclitus whose doctrine of flux and mutability always held him in thrall, well summarised in the fragment:

> One cannot step twice into the same river, nor can one grasp any mortal substance in a stable condition, but it scatters and again gathers; it forms and dissolves and approaches and departs.*

Sports, gardening, Scottish dancing and amateur dramatics also featured, maintaining an active social environment at the college. Graham acted in a production of Synge's *Riders of the Sea*; its themes of drowning and loss would soon haunt his poetry. And here it was he regularly serenaded his fellow students especially a lassie from Blantyre named Nessie Dunsmuir (nine years his senior), his future sweetheart and wife, although the relationship was not to blossom fully for some time. It would be no exaggeration to say that the experiences of Newbattle ignited Graham's passion for literature, as well as a philosophical proclivity, and focussed his determination to become a poet of probing integrity.

The outbreak of war in 1939 saw Graham hasten for a brief period to the west of Ireland to avoid conscription. There he worked on a farm and later at the Dublin docks. Returning to Scotland he submitted to a medical examination where an ulcer was diagnosed (they remained a lifelong concern) and he was given work at a torpedo factory at Fort Matilda. Graham was now fully devoted to his poetry in any spare time available.

The war years in Glasgow attracted an intriguing coterie of characters, some fleeing the horrors of Central Europe and others the London blitz. Amongst the latter was David Archer, a bookseller, philanthropist and patron. He had already published the first collections of Dylan Thomas, George Barker and David Gascoyne. Archer was a prime target for

Graham's pursuit in finding a publisher for his first collection *Cage Without Grievance*, which duly appeared under the wing of Archer's Parton Press in 1942.

A sprightly mix of writers, poets, artists, actors and musicians were all enticed to Archer's home at Sandyford Place and the Scott Street Art Centre, which he also set up. Amid this circle were the painters Robert Frame, Benjamin Creme, Robert Colquhoun and Robert MacBryde ('The two Roberts'), alongside the Polish refugees Josef Herman and Jankel Adler. These were the first real painters that Graham would get to know, and a strong case could certainly be made for Graham having more visual artists for soul mates than writers. Adler had known Paul Klee well and Graham now helped him with a translation of a significant article on Klee for *Horizon* magazine, claiming to have turned his Polish English into polished English (ever the compulsive punster). Adler's art, particularly his stylised faces, exerted some influence on Graham, evident in the many sketches and doodles decorating his letters. Adler's dedicated work ethic also proved exemplary.

Kilquhanity, a progressive school near Galloway, offered Graham some teaching work. Here he met and got seriously involved with a colleague Mary Harris. Her family owned two gypsy caravans in Germoe in Cornwall, located in Pengersick Lane which just happened to lead down to Sydney Cove, and the couple made the bold decision, in the summer of 1943, to move there to live the simple life. However, the partnership was short lived and soon the pregnant Harris chose to return to Scotland where she gave birth to their daughter, Rosalind.

We now see the beginning of Graham's self-imposed exile, almost as far as he could travel from his native corner of the British Isles to another Celtic corner. The free accommodation lured him there, but he also had a desire to distance himself, literally, from what he perceived to be an artificial and embarrassing attempt at the creation of a Scottish national literature under the aegis of Hugh MacDiarmid (though the two men remained friends).

Graham named the caravan The Wheelhouse, and it was from here that he embarked on the simple, frugal existence, without the demands or distractions of serious employment, necessitated by his total commitment to poetry, described in a letter to his old friend Edwin Morgan (22/9/1943):

The poet does not write what he knows but what he doesn't know. At this time I am more alive and creative in my thinking and intellect than I have ever been. I have read more, there are more things I am more sure of, I am more single and more constantly in my days a poet … My poems tell me and let me peer through to something real and more elemental which has to do with all I breathe and make and am made.

To earn a modest crust Graham tried living off the land, he grew violets for the London market, attempted, unsuccessfully, to ferret out rabbits and got the occasional labouring job digging potatoes.

Like many writers at this time the work he produced was dense in mixed metaphors, compound words and juxtaposed imagery, fuelled by Surrealism, Automatism and, inevitably, Dylan Thomas (all bouncing along on tautly sprung Hopkinsian rhythms). The result is an excessively rich plum cake difficult to chew on and well nigh impossible to swallow without choking. However, it's interesting that Graham always defended the early work and insisted it be included in his *Collected Poems*, almost forty-years later he wrote to Gavin Saunders (14/4/1981):

My early poems are as good as my later poems. They are maybe just not fashionable, but neither are my later poems. The early poems are other objects with their own particular energies. To say I am getting better, or have written myself into a greater clearness, is very much a surface observation.

Apart from the poetry Graham was always an intense correspondent, part of his essential armoury of communication in remoteness, and his many letters give the impression of a versatile wordsmith limbering up to the joyful cadences of language. Unlike the structural constraints of the poetry, his epistolary prose allowed total freedom for Graham's strong Joycean inclinations to let rip and test the elasticity of the language in an outrageously ludic vein.

In October 1943 he displayed a confident young man's audacity and admirable directness by writing to Ben Nicholson, then an artist of international repute living at Carbis Bay with Barbara Hepworth and their children (16/10/1943):

Dear Sir,
I'm living here near Praa Sands in a caravan a friend's lent me. I've been here three months and would like to talk to someone. I'm quite alone here.

Could I please visit you. I'm interested in poetry. Parton Press published my first book about a year ago. If it's all right will you let me know when to come. I can ride over on my bike.

Ben Nicholson

Unfortunately we have no record of this or subsequent meetings apart from a tantalising reference made by Nicholson in a letter to Herbert Read in May 1944 that he had recently seen Graham and, 'his method of working at his writing seems like my method of working at my painting.' Not many people would ever think of linking the two men and it remains intriguing that Graham was so keen to contact Nicholson.

1944 saw him joined by his old flame Nessie for another period of sharing their life together. The same year *The Seven Journeys* was published to poor reviews, with the pontificating shadow of Thomas cited as a jaundiced influence. The logomania of *Finnegans Wake* was also in the air and Graham possessed the pamphlet edition of *Anna Livia Plurabelle*, adding a further Celtic torque to his tongue.

During these war years he would sometimes hitchhike up to London where he was swayed into bibulous rovings in Fitzrovia, spilling drinks with his old cronies 'The two Roberts' as well as Dylan Thomas with whom he got on well. In fact Thomas really valued Graham's comments on drafts of his own work.

In his *Memoirs of the Forties* Julian Maclaren-Ross describes the mood of our Greenock man thus:

> *His expression was that of one stolidly bearing up under constant injustice or undeserved misfortune, and an atmosphere of brooding perpetually surrounded him. He sat over his beer as if reviewing every insult he had ever received with the purpose of devising effectual retorts for the future. In fact nobody insulted him at all and most people had a great respect for his poetry.*

He developed a close friendship with the neo-Romantic painter John Minton who was to visit him in Cornwall with Keith Vaughan. Graham wrote him many exuberant letters at this time (24/4/1945):

> *THE EAR SPEAKS MORE THAN THE TONGUE   LISTEN –*
> *Cornwall 24 4 45 after a wee shower gently upon my young friends new planted by the vanside … I'm making a new shithouse today and digging away like a steam shovel but my head buzzing with the ideas of the wide word world like any young girl enamoured with a big bunch of neuroses.*

In these letters to Minton we also see an emerging habit for requests for the loan of money to help him along; this would be a recurring sub-text to many of his correspondents.

Graham presently became friendly with the charismatic Sven Berlin, though he was not impressed on their first meeting (April/May 1945?):

> *We had a night out drinking with this man Sven Berlin who paints and writes and is having his book on Alfred Wallis published … He's pleasant and intelligent but knows fuckall about writing and painting. He has a moustache. He's just a big laddie of 32. He's nice but no great excitement to talk to.*

Nevertheless this encounter would prove fruitful as Berlin commissioned Graham to write a poem for his forthcoming book, the first ever study of the 'primitive' artist Alfred Wallis. As a seaman and self-taught outsider of innocent integrity, Wallis had an obvious appeal to the poet. 'The Voyages of Alfred Wallis' was finished in the autumn of 1945; Graham never got paid the promised fee but received a copy of the book instead. He wrote to Berlin saying he cut the pictures out to stick to the walls for a few days, 'then sticking them back neatly with tape' (7/3/1949).

He was also going through a phase of religious reading, including the Bible and John Donne's sermons. ('Also many books about Tibet. Tibet is a strange place and I read a lot about it.')

Furthermore Graham was attempting to set down in prose his own remarkable philosophy of poetry and poetics, which would soon be published in *Poetry Scotland* (July 1946) with the title 'Notes on a Poetry of Release'.* Here he sets out the credo, with its Heraclitean echoes, that would steer his whole writing life.

Selected quotations from 'Notes on a Poetry of Release':

The most difficult thing for me to remember is that a poem is made of words and not of the expanding heart, the overflowing soul, or the sensitive observer. A poem is made of words. It is words of a certain order, good or bad by the significance of its addition to life and not to be judged by any other value put upon it by imagining how or why or by what kind of man it was made. It is easy to strive to make a poem out of the wrong material like a table out of water. It is easy to mistake a poem for a different thing with a different function and to be sad when it does not put out what it is not …

For the language is a changing creature continually being killed-off, added-to and changed like a river over its changing speakers …

Each word changes every time it is brought to life. Each single word uttered twice becomes a new word each time. You cannot twice bring the same word into sound …

The poem is more than the poet's intention. The poet does not write what he knows but what he does not know …

The poem itself is dumb but has the power of release. Its purpose is that it can be used by the reader to find out something about himself … He must face it that words are ambiguous, but realise that this has to do with the fundamental force of poetry and is to be used to a positive end. The poem is not a handing out of the same packet to everyone, as it is not a thrown-down heap of words for us to choose the bonniest …

Let the poem be a still thing, a mountain constructed, an addition to the world. It will have its own special function and purpose, to be that certain mountain. And there is the reader going on to it with his never-before exploration after his perfect hunger's daily changing bread …

It is a good direction to believe that this language which is so scored and impressed by the commotion of all of us since its birth can be arranged to in its turn impress significantly for the benefit of each individual. Let us endure the sudden affection of the language.

The great care that Graham took in constructing a poem was noted later by George Barker when he described the work as: 'a marvellous branch of Glasgow engineering … as lucidly and imaginatively constructed as anything that ever emerged from Greenock shipyards. They will sail the world.' Over the decades visitors to the Graham household often noted how he kept words and phrases pinned to the walls on pieces of cardboard. This was all part of his essential *modus operandi*, and these were the components to be skilfully assembled into the final edifice of the poem.

Early in 1947, Frank Baker, author and organist, offered the couple the use of his cottage in Mevagissey for six months. (Though Graham said the area lacked the mystic feeling found around Land's End.) This brought the 'gypsy' life in the caravans to a close. At this time Mevagissey was a particularly busy fishing harbour, with The Ship Inn acting as social hub. Nessie and Sydney were soon joining in with the nightly singalongs, which led to Graham being invited to join a local fishing crew (he already had some experience of these activities from his early Greenock days), providing invaluable insight on a precarious way of life not lost on the poet.

Come the autumn he and Nessie agreed to a temporary separation, the reasons are unclear (they didn't meet up again for another six years). This was the beginning of a strange, peripatetic, but stimulating few years for Graham. He had a pleasant surprise when he was given an 'Atlantic Award in Literature' (funded by the Rockefeller Foundation). Following this the American academic and critic Vivienne Koch, who had been writing enthusiastically about his work, arranged for him to teach at New York University. He lectured on English literature: an odd mix of

D. H. Lawrence, Hardy, the Brontes, Fielding's *Moll Flanders*, and Joyce (*Finnegans Wake* and *Dubliners*). There was also time for various leisure activities including regular games of tennis, plus, inevitably, his discovery of potent American beverages, described in a letter to Mary Harris: 'I'm healthy though I've been on the drink quite a bit. What cocktails here, Martinis, Manhattans, Tom Collins, and all calculated to "disarrange the senses"' (17/7/1948). His relationship with Koch had also become quite intense. What a contrast to the previous few years in Cornwall.

While in the US he also received exciting news from Faber & Faber that they would publish his collection *The White Threshold*, with T. S. Eliot writing that he was 'considerably impressed'. He returned to Mevagissey after about nine months.

The new book was awash with salty allusions to the sea. Written in Joycean style, with the Bible and *Moby-Dick* in tow. A Scottish homesickness is keenly felt by the many place-names littered throughout the text, including: Greenock, Bothwell, Lanark, Shian, Gigha, Ben Cruachan, Ben Narnain, Clyde, Dechmont, and the river Calder; alongside Scots vocabulary and dialect: 'tig', 'linty', 'mavis', 'airts', 'bing', 'gowan', 'brae', 'burn', 'lythe', 'kern', 'kyle', and 'makar' (meaning 'poet', providing Graham with a pleasing pun).

Aside from his enthusiastic reading of Robert Graves' *The White Goddess*, 'the most stimulating book I've read in years', Graham was further stretching his sea legs on a very long poem that would bring a phase of his writing life to a culmination. His letters make many references to his ongoing struggle with the epic scale, and some exasperation is revealed to Sven Berlin (12/3/1949):

> This 'Nightfishing', because of its size, is a bit of a monster to finish off. So often I feel lost in the middle of it not able to get out and back from it and see it as one object. But the bugger shall be fucked into an organic whole all the same. Christ it will be good to get it finished.

He also looked to Berlin to provide him with some unexpected assistance (7/3/1949):

> Thanks for the white friends, certainly a Godsend or St Svensend … They go quickly. I've watched, as you advise, and haven't rushed them too much. They are a great help in putting in a really long stretch of time on the work – when that is specially needed.

The 'white friends' were Benzedrine tablets, of which Berlin got a weekly supply on prescription. Benzedrine had been used by bomber pilots during the war to help them stay awake and alert, just what Graham demanded for his own nocturnal flights of the imagination. However he did show startling signs of becoming dependent (12/3/1949):

> And the 50 were a great help and faded fast and I must, next time, remember to put those tiger glands on shorter rations. Do what you can, Sven, for at the moment they are a spare engine in this bull-shouldering sea. Again I've resorted to sniffing those bloody B.H.s and got my nostrils really buggered up and bleeding. What a mad business. Still, it is the right thing for this time.

He refers to Benzedrine inhalers, and as these grew weaker in potency they could be heated near a flame or preferably on a cooker in order to squeeze out an extra 'up'.

Graham spent some of the early part of 1950 in London when he had several meetings with Eliot. Later in the summer the painter Bryan Wynter (who was away for a few months) lent him the use of his cottage, the Carn, on the moors above Zennor. From this remote boulder-strewn location Graham wrote to his old Scottish friend and fellow poet Edwin Morgan, to whom he was often known as Joke Grim* (31/7/1950):

> I sit almost surrounded by 'standing stones', cromlechs, and grey piles of rock and grey 'drystane dykes' and (I do think I'm the last person to believe in a whimsy way about druid feeling about the landscape) do you know, Edwin, it feels early and Celtic and definitely Unenglish ... (where Christ knows what has been done in the name of Magic and Worship)

Late in September this period of reverie and reflection was brought to a painful halt, as he explained (writing from Truro hospital) to another Scottish writer, Moncrieff Williamson (11/10/1950):

> I saw few people, worked hard, tried my best to beat the damp and on a wild rainy night 3 weeks ago I walked 5 miles into St Ives to attend a birthday party and coming home I managed (don't ask me how) to fall off a roof 30 feet and land on concrete.
>   Well being as I have angels galore awatching over me and being the luckiest man in the world I only collected – 1) A smashed patella

(kneecap), 2) A split forehead (5 stitches) and 3) concussion ... I've had two operations and my kneecap's been removed ...

Having made a decent recovery Graham would spend the next few years unsettled, moving in with the writer Elisabeth Smart for a period (in fact he became besotted with her) before embarking on a reading tour of the US, at the invitation of Malcolm Brinnin, with the slightly odd pairing of Kathleen Raine and David Gascoyne. While there he took the opportunity, on two occasions, to meet Ezra Pound, then incarcerated in a psychiatric hospital in Washington D.C. ('We got on well and talked fairly technically, which he seemed to love.')

At last Graham's majestic 'The Nighfishing' broke cover in the journal *Botteghe Oscure* in 1951, a highly regarded poetry publication founded under the wealthy patronage of the perceptive Princess Marguerite Caetani, who subsequently invited Graham to stay at her mediaeval castle south of Rome.

Here we have one of the great sea poems in the language, but with a difference, as he later wrote to Charles Causley (23/6/1955):

I wanted to write about the sea and make it a grey green sea, not a chocolate box sea ... Leonardo da Vinci has curious drawings in his notebooks of poured water and its currents and momentums and storms and driven tides and in a way I wanted to use those kinds of very physical phenomena in whatever real action was represented. Because although I wanted to write about the sea it was not the sea only as an objective adventure (if there is such a thing) but as experience surrounding a deeper problem which everybody is concerned with.

I mean the essential isolation of man and the difficulty of communication.

The poem has an incantatory tone spoken in a trancelike voice. There is a strong allegorical feeling of a perilous journey, with an emphasis on the futility of attempting to catch the slipperiness of identity using the porous net of language. Writing to the bibliophile, collector and publisher Alan Clodd, he provides a reassessment of his poem (9/2/1955):

With all its mistakes and blemishes I think it is a knit object, an obstacle of communication, if you like, which has to be climbed over or gone round but not walked through. I think it just might make its wee disturbance in the language. I think (in a dramatic way) it makes a place, organic and believable, within its lines. What it will be to others I have no idea ... If it made somebody seasick (a good unliterary measurement) I would be pleased.

January 1953 saw Graham visiting Nessie in Paris where she was teaching at the Berlitz School. Their essential kinship reignited (just in time, as she was contemplating getting married to a wealthy Frenchman). Returning to England, and during another period of drifting, they wed in October 1954 at a registry office in her hometown of Blantyre. A few months later, in February 1955, Faber published the collection *The Nightfishing*. No doubt a great boost to Graham's confidence and ambitions, nevertheless it remains an anomaly of literary history that his next book did not appear for another fifteen years.

Although there was some talk of moving to the Western Isles of Scotland, the couple once again found themselves carried along on the ship of fate in a south-westerly direction, returning them to the familiar bearings of the Land's End peninsula. This was early in 1956 and it would surely have come as a big surprise to Graham if he'd known he would dwell in this far-flung corner of Cornwall for the remaining thirty years of his life.

Despite Graham's negative first impression of Berlin, the artist consistently proved very supportive to him. Though he had recently departed St Ives (having fallen out with the Penwith Society of Artists),* Berlin allowed the Grahams to stay in his cottage, Penderleath, at Cripplesease, just opposite The Engine Inn, while they searched for something more permanent. They didn't have to wait long before finding an old coastguard house to rent on the promontory of Gurnard's Head, so called from its resemblance to the fish (Graham jokingly referred to himself as 'the brain of Gurnard's Head'). The house lay down a dirt track inaccessible to vehicles; the interior was frugal in the extreme and without electricity. Paraffin was the source of cooking and light, and for heat anything that came to hand that would burn – often bits of jetsam found beachcombing nearby shores. In time some of this detritus ended up around the walls decorated by Graham, including sheets of broken glass, all featuring his stylised, Adleresque faces. Their lives were destined to be perpetually impecunious, but against all the odds they maintained an old world dignity. Graham once informed Clodd (9/2/1955):

I've always been frightened of the insidious anaesthetic of comfort and although I am far from being an ascetic by nature I've rather welcomed conditions in which I could not entirely forget the weather.

There was certainly no ignoring the weather in this exhilarating location on the edge of the world. Graham got some work as an auxiliary coastguard, marching off in all weathers, while Nessie watched his lantern gradually disappear along the precipitous cliff path down to a hut situated right on the tip of the headland. He once assisted in the rescue of a drowning man. Surprising that he noticed as the hut became a useful place to write from ('I'm here sitting up in this wee cabin and the wind shrieking my ears off'). Nessie also got seasonal employment working in St Ives hotels, getting the bus in each day.

One vital amenity that the pair managed to avail themselves of whenever opportunity arose was the Gurnard's Head Hotel, within manageable walking distance. There were countless late night sessions when Graham liked to give his singing voice a good airing. As well as popular ballads, he sang in a hybrid of Italo-Gaelic gibberish of his own invention. Impromptu plays were devised, sometimes with imaginary exotic locations, when everyone present was expected to contribute in some way, usually providing special effects with much howling, gurgling, screeching, and whistling. The place was run by Jimmy and Daphne Goodman, an eccentric couple who were sympathetic to the local artists and their ways, which was just as well. (Other essential watering holes in the area included The Tinner's Arms in Zennor and in St Ives The Sloop and The Castle Inn. The latter run by Endell Mitchell, brother of the sculptor Denis.)

Karl Weschke, Nancy Wynne-Jones, WSG, Nessie and Brian Wall in The Sloop

As luck would have it the local talent consisted of an embarrassment of riches. The 1950s and early 1960s, in and around St Ives, are now perceived to have been a golden era in British art. Apart from Hepworth and Nicholson, there was also Peter Lanyon, Patrick Heron, Bryan Wynter, Terry Frost, Roger Hilton, Trevor Bell, Karl Weschke, Tony O'Malley, Wilhelmina Barns-Graham, Alan Lowndes, Nancy Wynne-Jones, Bill Featherston, Anthony Benjamin, Brian Wall to name a few. There was also the painter and sculptor Michael Snow who, 40 years later, would co-edit, with his wife Margaret, the important volume of Graham's letters. The Grahams were to rely heavily on the benevolence of many of these people over the coming decades.

For whatever reasons, Graham had detached himself from his native Scotland as well as divorcing himself from the literary opportunities on offer in London. He had chosen to live a materially meagre existence in a remote Celtic peninsula, but, ironically, it was here he found his 'aloneness' participating within a unique company of creative independent spirits. There was never a coherent St Ives group of artists with a program or manifesto, but a community of outsiders drawn, for a variety of reasons, to live and work on the edge of society in an elemental wilderness encompassed by the sea, as well as the inimitable light and sense of space. (It's also a land littered with the vestiges of human activity from Neolithic stone circles, through Iron Age field patterns, to the haunting ruins of the industrial revolution.) Many of these individuals were highly intelligent, displaying varying degrees of eccentricity, who had embarked on their own solo journeys of self-exploration through the visual arts. Not content with the etiquette of the picturesque they offered a challenge to the mind's eye, attempting to break habits of seeing, drawing on Constructivism, Abstract Expressionism, Cubism, Surrealism, or just the plain bizarre. Graham will undoubtedly have picked up many cues from their shared conversations on how he might, by the same token, 'disturb the language' by way of reconfiguring the words and syntax on the page. He may well have envied the plasticity of their medium allowing marks and strokes on the surface of the canvas, or whatever, to exist without the accumulated burdens of cliché and restricted meaning that had become attached, like barnacles, to words and phrases.

Though one of Graham's closest friends at this time was decidedly non-abstract. Alan Lowndes was a Stockport man of stammering truculence with a fierce thirst. His work drew from a northern working class background showing ordinary people going about the daily grind in a 'naïve' style that has a superficial resemblance to L. S. Lowry. Whenever he and Graham decided to pop out for a quick pint it would regularly turn into a 48-hour bender, much to the chagrin of Lowndes' wife Valerie and their children. But Lowndes displayed the kind of lively, independence of mind that Graham found stimulating.

WSG by Alan Lowndes, 1960

23

Alan Lowndes in The Tinner's Arms, Zennor, 1961

MADRON   I AM FIFTY TODAY   19 11 68   WE FALL
DOWN DARKNESS IN A LINE OF DESIRE AND FRUSTRATION TO
WHEREVER WE FALL DOWN TO AND THE DAYS LOOK IN THROUGH
THE WINDOW AND HARK HARK THE DOGS DO BARK MEASURELESS

Dear Rog dear Roger Dear CBE are you there?   I am a
brave man in my way but when one is a brave man in one's
way one is not a brave man in another.   With all my
sense of the comic in life, which means a certain sense of
proportion about reality, I know myselfe less and less and
wonder where it is I want to go.   We are each, in our own
respective ways, blessed or cursed with with certain
ingredients to help us for good or bad on our ways which
we think are our ways.   What's buzzin couzzin? Love thou
me?   When the idea of the flood had abated a hare pussed
in the shaking bell-flowers and prayed to the rainbow through
the spider's web.   I have my real fire on. I am on.

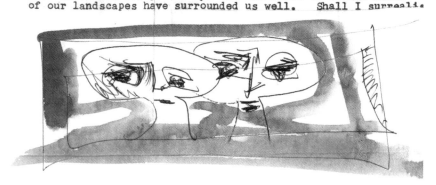

I miss you.   There must be a way to say 'Imiss you.' to
another man which has nothing to do with suggestions of homo
and is dignified and vital.   No harder man than me will
you possibly encounter.   I dont mean you should come back
necessarrily.   Maybe your time in Botallack is finished. You
must change gear now, my dear.   Your times in all your
mighty times is here.   It should be a 'changing-of-gear time.
You are too good to let things slide at the moment. There,
old fellow, Great Dog You, you have the power.   Put it out.
You and I have had some times of valuable Hell together. I
have affection for you always and the manic or serene hills
of our landscapes have surrounded us well.   Shall I surrealia

24

WSG letter to Roger Hilton

(HOW DOES ONE BEGIN?)   It is my house here with those
simple oils of lamps lit.   The door which will not shut is
my friend and outside there is a sea of silent safety pins
and a small sun rising to shine its rays on whoever I would
like to become.   I sit on the top of an igloo of ice and
inside is Mozart kept alive and I will not pretend I know
him well.

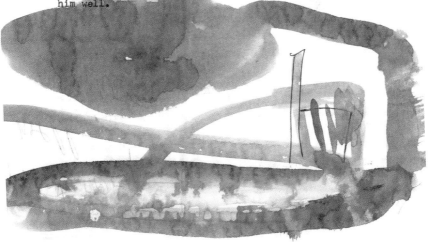

And so we leave this paradise wher the poet lives and have
had our wee spell there.   To tell you the honest truth,
I cant bear anybody.   Away and boil.   But of course, I
realise, I must keep somebody liking me a wee bit. Otherwise, where would I be at all.   WE MUST BE LIKED BY SOME
OTHER PERSON OR PERSONS SOMEWHERE IN THE WORLD.   Please
let me hear from you now as the light is failing at the
window and the road outside is quiet and the wind is sailing
the very unhuman rooks up over the chimney.   Love your friend.

                cheerio,

                    Sydney x

ater in 1956 Graham visited Patrick Heron, also newly arrived in the
area, at his impressive house, Eagle's Nest, overlooking Zennor village. It was here that he first encountered Roger Hilton and there
was an immediate intense rapport between the two men. A strange love-
hate relationship developed and many eyewitness accounts speak of the
toxicity of the atmosphere that could develop if the drink wasn't kept in
check. Hilton was legendary for his short fuse, impatience and personally
offensive behaviour fuelled by his addiction to whisky. At first they clearly
had a lot to offer each other by way of exchanging ideas. (Our record of
their friendship is regrettably one-sided. Whereas Hilton seems to have
kept most of the letters he received from Graham, Graham rarely kept any
correspondence and Hilton's carefully articulated letters were probably
used to light the fire.) In December 1956 Graham wrote about their meeting with great gusto (13/12/1956):

> The strange thing is this, Roger, I found when I returned here that your
> pictures and 'timbre of voice' of your painting had affected me more
> strongly than I had realised. In the same way as one sees influences of
> contemporary abstract painting in Landscape and in News photographs
> in newspapers lying upside down etc., that particular kind of graphic dis-
> turbance which is your 'voice' in painting suggested itself more and more
> in things …
>
> So, Roger, my love-chasing abstract boy, my hero of the graphic plain,
> my boy alone and lost in the disguising angers and rudenesses and pre-
> cipitations of catastrophe, my touchy switherer and buttery-fingered
> bearer of your self-esteem, artist of the astringent, the uncharming, the
> unkitchened, the unpotted and panned regions of the great proportions
> and intercoursing areas of light trying the eye, hurry up and come down
> soon … Shall I compare thee to a day of storms. Batter my Gurnard's
> Head. The wind roars and the waves rumble in …

At this time Hilton was living in London with his musician wife Ruth
and their children, but he hired various studios over the next few years in
St Ives and Newlyn when he would visit for weeks at a time.

Heron made this eloquent assessment, as early as 1952:

> Hilton begins and ends with paint. His whole system of pictorial thought
> and emotion is centred in his brush strokes themselves. The precise char-
> acter, the texture, size, colour, tone, direction and rhythm of each ragged
> touch is his main conscious preoccupation. And this is why he is abstract.

The quality of his paint surface fills his conscious mind and, thus obtruding, prevents him seeing round or beyond it to the need for a subject. Nevertheless, what we call 'the subject' is something eternally present in visual art. It is an element no conscious effort on the abstract artist's part can succeed in eliminating ...*

In other words, Hilton had a more technical, academic approach that saw the painting as a self-contained object with its own self-referential rules of coherence based on colour and form without external referents. (Though the viewer would often impose some pattern unbeknown to the artist.) He once remarked about the surrounding Cornish landscape: 'Thank God I can enjoy it without thinking how to paint it.' Later on his work became more quasi-representative, but for now he agonised over his struggle with the aesthetically hazardous tasks he set himself: 'The abstract artist submits himself entirely to the unknown ... he is like a man swinging out into the void.'

Hilton's philosophy clearly had appeal for Graham wrestling with his own very different objects and it was certainly a part of their mutual dependence to exchange the torments of the act of creation (26/9/1968):

As usual I am worried about my fucking poetry, not wanting to jump onto the wagon of the prevailing style and yet not wanting to stick with a texture of words which is rigidly me. To be new in the right way is difficult, not to put out suedo (sic) experimental confections ... As you say about the oblique look at the art object one must not frighten it away by facing it too blatantly yet somehow know the particular quality of its mystery and do all the things to encourage itself to 'grow'.

Hilton moved permanently down to Cornwall in 1965 setting up home at Botallack with his new wife Rose and their two boys. Ultimately the relationship with Graham proved to be a kind of fatal attraction, causing suffering to all who happened to get caught in the crossfire. The fact that Graham had an affair with Ruth – Hilton's ex-wife – was another volatile ingredient complicating the mix.

Ruth, as a professional viola player, also ministered to Graham's creativity. Since his childhood singing days he always took a serious interest in music, and the radio tuned to classical music was hardly ever off in the Graham household. He never ceased to be awed by this technology, as he related to Ruth (13/10/1966):

I've put an aerial on my Marconi invention and the music programme is louder and clearer. What a great invention it is. I still am able to think of it as freshly as the desert island savage. How does art be able to come through the empty spaces, the whirling spaces of air, through the walls and over the mountains?

WSG and Tim Dolan

He had many lengthy conversations with Ruth about the technicalities of music and it was she who lent him the book *On Playing the Flute* by the 18th century composer Johann Joachim Quantz. Graham's close study of this manual gave birth to his fine poem 'Johann Joachim Quantz's Five Lessons' (where he adopted its pedantic tone almost verbatim). He often had musical arrangement in mind when writing and once remarked that 'The Dark Dialogues' were akin to a Beethoven quartet. He dropped more clues about the role of patterns of sound in an interview with John Haffenden:

I will tell you, if there is one way I differ from perhaps most other poets, it is because I write in verse with a distinct rhythm. I mean, we have all read what Eliot says about vers libre; *it's something I'm not very happy with, although I do like Pound. I need to know where I am, counting out my lines inside myself – as though a metronome were going – to allow myself to make things within the beat, which of course makes rhythmic shapes more easy to do. If you don't get the beat established silently in the centre of the words and within the words' sense you can't make anything which goes out from the rhythmic beat.*

I'd like to have my poems set to music, and I'd dearly love to write a song cycle. It's one of the sadnesses of my life that I didn't apply myself to knowing the language of how to set down music.

Roger and Rose Hilton at home at Botallack, 1972

Meanwhile, back at Gurnard's Head the Grahams were clearly struggling under difficult living conditions, with Nessie often ill. Neighbours noticed that they appeared malnourished and seemed to be living on nettle soup. A degree of their pauperism can be glimpsed in a letter to the psychologist and painter Marie Singer in early 1958 (27/1/1958):

The news of the sweet shirt and the bonny jeans is great for the ones I have (my only trousers) are worn thin as pyjamas and anyway were always at halfmast ... Now please forgive me asking a gift horse for another but I may as well ask you this in case you know of someone. I'm terribly desperate for a pair of shoes or boots and when I've been writing my friends I've been asking them if they have any old pair which they have finished with and which, although not wearable in town, would keep my poor iambic feet off the flint of Cornwall.

However, a significant new 'guardian angel' was about to enter the lives of Sydney and Nessie Graham, offering some degree of redemption in the form of the artist Nancy Wynne-Jones. Wynne-Jones was a Welsh heiress who moved to St Ives in 1957 to study painting under Peter Lanyon. She then lived at the Battery on the Island overlooking Porthmeor Beach. She was one of the few artists to have money and was always a very generous host. She kept an open house where visitors could be confident of making merry and enjoy the rare pleasure of having a glass never less than half full.

Graham had already experienced something of Wynne-Jones' patronage when she paid for him to travel to Iceland in 1961. (This trip related to his favourite reading about Arctic exploration.) In 1962 she bought, with the potter Boots Redgrave, a large country house at Trevaylor near the

Bill Featherston at Trevaylor

village of Gulval, between Zennor and Penzance. The house was mainly 18th century but parts of it were Elizabethan and it included fine gardens with stables and barns, which were converted into studios. She took pity on the Grahams and invited them to live there for free. Several other artists moved in including Tony O'Malley* and Bill Featherston (a sculptor from Toronto working in a variety of media. Another big drinking buddy, years later Featherston would play host to Graham when he visited Canada). Wynne-Jones soon bought the lodge opposite the big house and the Grahams settled in there, calling it Woodfield.

Despite the newly found relative comfort of being looked after, this came at a price for the couple as Graham became romantically involved with Wynne-Jones. Nessie was still travelling in to St Ives daily for work leaving Graham at home with temptation more or less on the doorstep.

The intensity and proximity of the affair could also partly explain Graham's low output as a poet over these years. It eventually came to an end when Wynne-Jones met the Irish sculptor Conor Fallon in 1965 (they married the following year).

In 1964 Wynne-Jones took the Grahams on holiday to Crete that led to an ongoing fascination for Graham with the island and he spent years reworking a long poem 'The Dream of Crete'; it exists in several drafts but was never completed.

The same year disaster hit the whole community of St Ives with the sudden death of Peter Lanyon. He was one of the few artists

WSG and Nancy Wynne-Jones, 1958

of this period actually from the place. He was a proud tough Cornishman who could be impatient with the mass of blow-ins colonizing the small town. Lanyon made a virtue of physically interacting with the elemental wilderness of Cornwall in all its dramatic humours. His work presented a challenge to the act of seeing, discarding a fixed viewpoint, and bringing a visceral energy and gesture to getting under the skin of a place, to uncover primal layers of history. He took up gliding to experience a vertiginous perspective on the land as well as expose himself to the atmospheric forces of the weather.

For many people Lanyon was the dynamo of the St Ives art community and for them something significant died with him and the place never felt the same again. Graham responded to this tragedy with 'The Thermal Stair', one of his finest poems.*

By the mid-sixties Trevaylor had gradually become colonised by an awful lot of time-wasters and hangers-on and had acquired a somewhat notorious reputation amongst the locals. Wynne-Jones eventually had a bust up with Redgrave and the house was sold. In 1967 she made the benevolent gesture of buying a small terrace house at 4 Mount View in Madron for the Grahams to move into and live rent-free. Directly opposite the local graveyard, their house was not far from the poorhouse where Wallis had died in 1942; which in turn had become a home for the elderly before becoming a slaughterhouse (for animals), a sequence of utility not

WSG and Tony O'Malley

WSG by Tony O'Malley

33

lost on Graham. There was also a handy local in The King William IV where Graham liked to sit at lunchtime attending to his correspondence.

A small steady body of work had been slowly emerging over the 15 years since *The Nightfishing*, and Graham's poems turned up from time to time in various poetry and other journals (often in America). But the literary world was in for a big surprise early in 1970 when Faber launched *Malcolm Mooney's Land* (He often referred to his publisher as Fibber & Fibber). Through the protracted silence many people had assumed Graham was dead.

As a reminder of his existence he provided this note regarding his new book for the *Poetry Book Society Bulletin* (Spring 1970):

> *Thoughts of the process of making poetry are often the subject of my poems, although I hope the poem is left standing in its own right apart from any takeawayable message the reader might discover.*
>
> *I happen to feel most alive when I am trying to write poetry. So here I am battering against the door in case there might be somebody behind it.*
>
> *I am always very aware that my poem is not a telephone call. The poet only speaks one way. He hears nothing back. His words as he utters them are not conditioned by a real ear replying from the other side. That is why he has to make the poem stand stationary as an Art object. He never knows who will collide with it and maybe even use it as a different utensil from what he intended. Yet because I am only human, I hope I am in it somewhere.*

The title poem was written in the form of a diary by an explorer lost in the Arctic. Graham loved books of travel (and had a predilection for the stark, icy lexicon of polar exploration); he particularly admired Fridtjof Nansen both as a man and a writer (his great memoir is *Farthest North*). The collection emphasises the ongoing problem of language as a necessary means of communication, while simultaneously proving to be an obstacle to, or at least a distortion of the veracity of that communication. In turn, this uncertainty undermines our very sense of identity. These poems can be regarded as meta-poetry in that the language of the poem turns in on itself as the words interrogate each other; this brings to mind the mythical uruborus, the snake eating its own tail. Graham will have seen enough abstract art around him to understand that these paintings create their own space, their own sense of place within the frame. They are not paintings of anything 'out there'. Even though they have to extract, to some extent, from an 'objective' reality they undergo a transformation becoming a unique independent object in their own right, just like a Graham poem. Space and silence correspond in the poem 'The Constructed Space': 'I say this silence or, better, construct this space/So that somehow something may move across/The caught habits of language to you and me.'

He noted the response to the new book in a letter to Charles Monteith, editor at Faber (14/10/1970):

> As you will have seen MALCOLM MOONEY'S LAND has called forth a mixed batch of reviews. The worst are vicious while the best are filled with passionate acclaim. Taking them all together I think there are more thumbs up than down. It is strange, Charles, that my verse (or the kind of man I am) either riles or is taken on its own scale at its best.

During the same year he had a nice surprise, as he wrote to the poet and critic Robin Skelton (7/5/1970):

> I have just had word that the Scottish Arts Council have awarded me £300. That is an inside WC on to our house. I am very pleased. It is a wee bit recognition from Scotland at last. I have always been a wee bit hurt (JOKE OR NOT JOKE?) that Scotland have never said anything about their exiled boy here, me. Also they have invited me up to do some readings in June or July in Edinburgh, Glasgow, and Stirling at the new University. I am very happy about it.

His distant homeland continued to nag away at Graham's conscience, though a sense of ambivalence also remained to badger him, as he explained to William Montgomerie (24/9/1969):

> Have I given up Scotland? Not that I know. I certainly couldn't write the poems I do without being Scots. Of course I have great bouts of homesickness for Scotland, the land and the people. But the selfconsciousness of what the Scottish art scene seems to be today embarrasses me tae hell.

November 1973 saw Graham doing a reading tour of Canada. Travelling alone, he stayed with several old friends including Bill and Gail Featherston as well as Skelton. It was not an unqualified success as some of the letters reveal. There was also drama on the return flight, as he reported to the Featherstons (4/12/1973):

I was very ill on the plane and I really thought I was finished. They gave me oxygen which didn't work because they found the oxygen bottle was empty. I gasped from Montreal to over Ireland. I was taken to hospital for two hours near London Airport and I could hardly remember where I had come from ... I stayed there in bed for two days. They gave me an injection and Mogadon and I slept for about 14 hours, the first good sleep for days. It was something to do with the heart. OK OK. A long rigmarole but, Bill, Gail, I thought I was off down the manhole leaving Ness and my cat to face the world alone.

Graham's recuperation was aided by the news, in January 1974, that he had been awarded a Civil List pension of £500 a year, a considerable boost to their otherwise life of penury. Skelton was a hugely important benefactor for Graham, and it was thanks to his efforts that the pension came about. Also for many years he had been sending Graham money in exchange for manuscripts (now housed in the archives of the University of Victoria, Canada), and regularly published Graham's poems in his journal *The Malahat Review*.

Bryan Wynter was a popular man amongst all those who knew him. He had arrived in Cornwall immediately after the war (he'd been a registered Conscientious Objector), intent on starting his artistic life afresh in a simple remote location. He soon acquired the remote Carn Cottage high on the moors overlooking Zennor village. In the 1950s he began experimenting with how mescaline might affect his painting. He produced large canvasses of shimmering intensity and depth, fuelled by surroundings of wild moorland and cliffs. In a catalogue for a 1962 exhibition he explained:

These paintings, then, are not pure abstractions. Nor do I abstract from 'nature'. I approach 'nature' from the other side.
I used to be an abstract painter. Am I still influenced by landscape? The landscape I live among is bare of houses, trees, people; is dominated by winds, by swift changes of weather, by the moods of the sea; sometimes it is devastated and blackened by fire. These elemental forces enter the paintings and lend their qualities without becoming motifs.

Graham met Wynter soon after the artist's arrival. Their rapport was instant, they shared an outrageous and mischievous sense of humour and great love of sophisticated (and sometimes dreadful) puns. When the Grahams lived at Gurnard's Head, Wynter would signal to them with mirrors from his cottage, several miles away, across the Zennor hills. They liked to make up plays together and also play at movie making (without any cameras). Graham's poem 'Wynter and the Grammarsow' displays this activity as a film script, with the words 'sound' and 'cut' interspersed throughout. Wynter was always very generous to the Grahams, even passing on old clothes, their tailoring was, in the main, compatible (25/9/1974):

Dear Brrryan,
Thanks for the trousers. I think they will fit me well except maybe the ballroom is not my own. Somewhere our belonging parts believe in us. If we could only find them.

Wynter had a serious heart attack as far back as 1961 and had recovered well (with Monica and their two boys he had moved to a house out near St Buryan in 1964). On 9 February 1975, while changing a puncture on his mini, he had another heart attack and seemed to have survived again; he died two days later.

Graham was devastated, as he wrote to Skelton (9/2/1975, incorrectly dated):

It is morning, Robin, and I am very drunk.
Bryan Wynter died last night. Whether you knew him or not does not matter. I could have got drunk for any simple reason. He happened to be a man who was very near me in my life for about 30 years. I can't believe it. This is not a letter to tell you somebody has died. You don't know him anyhow. But here I am up in the early Madron morning drunk as a handcart or any adjective you may choose wanting to tell you that he will never come into the house again tapping at the back window. I can't believe it. But here we are, Robin, still going through our lives as we respectively do.

As if this major personal loss were not enough, Roger Hilton died just twelve days later. Graham and Hilton had drifted apart a few years earlier. Though Graham was always a heavy drinker he was nowhere in the same league as Hilton's addictive consumption of daily bottles of whisky that, inevitably, destroyed his health. For the last few years of his life he was bedridden, attended to by his long-suffering and magnanimous wife, Rose. Once again (or twice again if you like) Graham's deep affection and tenderness for his old friends motivated him to turn to the elegy, in its intimate epistolary form, to articulate his deprivation, leaving us with 'Dear Bryan Wynter' and 'Lines on Roger Hilton's Watch.'

He wrote to the poet C. H. Sisson (11/3/1975):

I have lost two very near people in my life suddenly in one week with no chance of preparation. Bryan Wynter and Roger Hilton. A year or two older than me. It is as though my very awareness of the world has been put out a bit and my thoughts from now on will be different. I am missing them going though their ups and down just a few parishes away.

Monica and Bryan Wynter in the frame at the Carn

38

Ronnie Duncan was another long standing friend and benefactor to Graham. They shared a great fascination with the history and landscape of Crete. Duncan and his wife Henriette took the Grahams there for a holiday in May 1977. But Graham was not at his best, indeed far from it and the trip certainly strained their affinity. However, Duncan's love for the man overrode the difficulties and the relationship remained steadfast. This was often the case with Graham and certain of his friendships, people tolerated some anti-social behaviour because of a deep respect for his unwavering integrity as a writer. There was also an inherent shyness he attempted to disguise with a certain belligerent swagger not always appreciated by those who didn't know him well.

During the 1960s Graham's output had been somewhat erratic with difficult periods of inertia. Now he was flying along as can be seen in many letters over this decade where he consistently talks of how well he's writing, from his little cottage in Madron. 1977 saw Faber publish *Implements in Their Places*. Once again Graham provided a note for *Poetry Book Society Bulletin* (Autumn 1977):

> *I can discern maybe an effort somewhere to try to be more simple or, if you will, less confused by the English language. But the word 'simple' is difficult either applied to lines of words on the page or to the thought which provoked them. Maybe this book is going to be more entertaining to more people. Is that what I want? After speaking to myself I suppose I want to speak to the best, whoever they are, alive or dead.*

As well as the usual concerns about language, well exemplified in the poem 'What is the Language Using Us For?', there were poems offering a strong sense of local place ('Enter a Cloud', 'Two Poems on Zennor Hill'), and an increased number of poems harking back to Graham's Scottish childhood, the places he grew up, and a moving poem to his father. As he grew older the homesickness bit deeper. He wrote to Duncan, in a tone of some urgency (28 July 1979):

> *Ronnie,*
> *I want to be back. I want to be back.*
>   *I want to be back with Ness somewhere in Scotland. Surely you can get some place. I have now had my fill of away.*
>   *The point is give us a wee place to finish in, in Scotland. I feel my life is finished here and I need to get back. Try your best.*

Graham's 're-discovery' was now gathering some momentum, and the publication of *Collected Poems 1942-1977* rapidly followed in 1979. He received prestigious awards from various organisations, including the Arts Council of Great Britain and the Royal Literary Fund. This recognition offered him some solace after decades of disregard.

The demand for public readings all over Britain also increased, which led to him visiting Scotland at last, in 1981, and performing in Edinburgh, Glasgow and Dundee. As a reader his performances varied considerably. At his best he could hold an audience enthralled with a commanding presence, exploring every syllable of a poem as if for the first time in a hushed atmosphere. On the other hand he liked to have a drink to steady his nerves before a reading and, depending on the company, he could overdo it resulting in an evening of anarchy. The anxious organisers of these events could never be sure of what to expect.

Unfortunately Graham's health was now in rapid decline. There were periods of depression, shared with Nessie, when neither of them would answer the door to any visitors. (Throughout these dark days the Grahams were grateful for some local practical help from Hilda and Albert Strick.) In 1984 and the following year he underwent operations for cancer, weakening him considerably and no more engagements were undertaken. Eventually, on the morning of 9 January 1986, in the little Madron cottage, he yielded his final breath to the world.*

S ydney Graham was a vivid character making a considerable impact on all those who knew him. Not all of the St Ives artists got on with him, though most did, but all of them certainly looked to him, with some degree of awe, as an exemplar how an artist of caliber should stand firm (convinced of his calling) and steer his life with courage. As the painters' various styles and credos surely influenced him as a writer, in turn Graham influenced them as role model. His was a lonely role, being the only writer of stature in such a fertile community of creative spirits (which is a surprise in itself). Visitors were usually asked to read his poems aloud to him (a nerve wracking experience for some people), as he was desperate to hear an echo from the void into which he had first sent them out. Graham never stopped pushing the boundaries of his art even though it remained a perpetual challenge, as he wrote to Skelton (8/12/1972):

What a mysterious, unsubstantial business it is, writing poetry. After one finishes a poem which seems to work one says Ha Ha now I'll write another because I know how to do it but it is not so. There is the silence before one just as difficult to disturb significantly as before. What one has learned is inadequate against the new silence presented. WOW!

Graham was a philosophical poet whose work has a strong appeal to the mind's ear. Most of what he read had to do with ideas: there was a good deal of philosophy including Schopenhauer, Hegel and Heidegger, amongst the many travel books Darwin's *Voyage of the Beagle*, and in poetry he was partial to a master of artifice like Marianne Moore; he rarely read fiction.

He never lost his Scottish accent. Even at its most monosyllabic and paired down, perhaps especially so, his voice sounds Scots (similarly Beckett, for all his silences and pauses, maintained an Irish brogue). Despite the verbal wrestling with linguistic abstractions, time and again his work remained anchored in place, both Scotland and Cornwall; as he mentioned in a late letter to the journalist Frank Ruhrmund (6/12/1984):

I am very pleased when Nessie tells me you said 'It is Graham country' when you were up at Gurnard's Head. In a kind of way there is a great deal of this place in my poems.

Three decades on from Graham's death his work transcends all national or place specific boundaries and continues to enunciate, with considerable resonance, the deepest concerns of the human quest for meaning in a universe of silence.

WSG at Gurnard's Head, 1958

Poems for Four Painters

WSG by Bill Featherston

THE VOYAGES OF ALFRED WALLIS

Worldhauled, he's grounded on God's great bank,
Keelheaved to Heaven, waved into boatfilled arms,
Falls his homecoming leaving that old sea testament,
Watching the restless land sail rigged alongside
Townful of shallows, gulls on the sailing roofs.
And he's heaved once and for all a high dry packet
Pecked wide by curious years of a ferreting sea,
His poor house blessed by very poverty's religious
Breakwater, his past house hung in foreign galleries.
He's that stone sailor towering out of the cupboarding sea
To watch the black boats rigged by a question quietly
Ghost home and ask right out the jackets of oil
And standing white of the crew 'what hellward harbour
Bows down her seawalls to arriving home at last?'

Falls into home his prayerspray. He's there to lie
Seagreat and small, contrary and rare as sand.
Oils overcome and keep his inward voyage.
An Ararat shore, loud limpet stuck to its terror,
Drags home the bible keel from a returning sea
And four black shouting steerers stationed on movement
Call out arrival over the landgreat houseboat.
The ship of land with birds on seven trees
Calls out farewell like Melville talking down on
Nightfall's devoted barque and the parable whale.
What shipcry falls? The holy families of foam
Fall into wilderness and 'over the jasper sea'.
The gulls wade into silence. What deep seasaint
Whispered this keel out of its element?

The Thermal Stair

For the painter Peter Lanyon killed in a gliding accident 1964

I called today, Peter, and you were away.
I look out over Botallack and over Ding
Dong and Levant and over the jasper sea.

Find me a thermal to speak and soar to you from
Over Lanyon Quoit and the circling stones standing
High on the moor over Gurnard's Head where some

Time three foxglove summers ago, you came.
The days are shortening over Little Parc Owles.
The poet or painter steers his life to maim

Himself somehow for the job. His job is Love
Imagined into words or paint to make
An object that will stand and will not move.

Peter, I called and you were away, speaking
Only through what you made and at your best.
Look, there above Botallack, the buzzard riding

The salt updraught slides off the broken air
And out of sight to quarter a new place.
The Celtic sea, the Methodist sea is there.

    You said once in the Engine
    House below Morvah
    That words make their world
    In the same way as the painter's
    Mark surprises him
    Into seeing new.
    Sit here on the sparstone
    In this ruin where
    Once the early beam
    Engine pounded and broke
    The air with industry.

    Now the chuck of daws
    And the listening sea.

'Shall we go down' you said
'Before the light goes
And stand under the old
Tinworkings around
Morvah and St Just?'
You said 'Here is the sea
Made by alfred wallis
Or any poet or painter's
Eye it encountered.
Or is it better made
By all those vesselled men
Sometime it maintained?
We all make it again'.

Give me your hand, Peter,
To steady me on the word.

Seventy-two by sixty,
Italy hangs on the wall.
A woman stands with a drink
In some polite place
And looks at SARACINESCO
And turns to mention space.
That one if she could
Would ride Artistically
The thermals you once rode.

Peter, the phallic boys
Begin to wink their lights.
Godrevy and the Wolf
Are calling Opening Time.
We'll take the quickest way
The tin singers made.
Climb here where the hand
Will not grasp on air.
And that dark-suited man
Has set the dominoes out
On the Queen's table.
Peter, we'll sit and drink

And go in the sea's roar
To Labrador with wallis
Or rise on Lanyon's stair.

Uneasy, lovable man, give me your painting
Hand to steady me taking the word-road home.
Lanyon, why is it you're earlier away?
Remember me wherever you listen from.
Lanyon, dingdong dingdong from carn to carn.
It seems tonight all Closing bells are tolling
Across the Duchy shire wherever I turn.

LINES ON ROGER HILTON'S WATCH

Which I was given because
I loved him and we had
Terrible times together.

O tarnished ticking time
Piece with your bent hand,
You must be used to being
Looked at suddenly
In the middle of the night
When he switched the light on
Beside his bed. I hope
You told him the best time
When he lifted you up
To meet the Hilton gaze.

I lift you up from the mantel
Piece here in my house
Wearing your verdigris.
At least I keep you wound
And put my ear to you
To hear Botallack tick.

You realise your master
Has relinquished you
And gone to lie under
The ground at St Just.

Tell me the time. The time
Is Botallack o'clock.
This is the dead of night.

> He switches the light on
> To find a cigarette
> And pours himself a Teachers.
> He picks me up and holds me
> Near his lonely face
> To see my hands. He thinks
> He is not being watched.

The images of his dream
Are still about his face
As he spits and tries not
To remember where he was.

I am only a watch
And pray time hastes away.
I think I am running down.

Watch, it is time I wound
You up again. I am
Very much not your dear
Last master but we had
Terrible times together.

Dear Bryan Wynter

1

This is only a note
To say how sorry I am
You died. You will realise
What a position it puts
Me in. I couldn't really
Have died for you if so
I were inclined. The carn
Foxglove here on the wall
Outside your first house
Leans with me standing
In the Zennor wind.

Anyway how are things?
Are you still somewhere
With your long legs
And twitching smile under
Your blue hat walking
Across a place? Or am
I greedy to make you up
Again out of memory?
Are you there at all?
I would like to think
You were all right
And not worried about
Monica and the children
And not unhappy or bored.

2

Speaking to you and not
Knowing if you are there
Is not too difficult.
My words are used to that.
Do you want anything?
Where shall I send something?
Rice-wine, meanders, paintings

By your contemporaries?
Or shall I send a kind
Of news of no time
Leaning against the wall
Outside your old house.

The house and the whole moor
Is flying in the mist.

3

I am up. I've washed
The front of my face.
And here I stand looking
Out over the top
Half of my bedroom window.
There almost as far
As I can see I see
St Buryan's church tower.
An inch to the left, behind
That dark rise of woods,
Is where you used to lurk.

4

This is only a note
To say I am aware
You are not here. I find
It difficult to go
Beside Housman's star
Lit fences without you.
And nobody will laugh
At my jokes like you.

5

Bryan, I would be obliged
If you would scout things out
For me. Although I am not
Just ready to start out.
I am trying to be better,

Which will make you smile
Under your blue hat.

I know I make a symbol
Of the foxglove on the wall.
It is because it knows you.

Notes

(Numbers indicate pages with *)

8: Kahn, C. H. *The Art & Thought of Heraclitus*. Cambridge University Press, 1981

13: Reprinted in *The Nightfisherman*.

16: Other nicknames, self-chosen, included Jocky Gramfunny, Juke Grumf, Wullie Grum, Troubleyouas Greyhim, Sadknee Graham.

18: Berlin's colourful non-conformist character didn't always harmonize with the Penwith Society of Artists. In 1962 he published *The Dark Monarch*, a *roman à clef* satirizing some of the artists and writers from his St Ives period. This attempt at some kind of revenge backfired big time when the publisher was quickly issued with four libel writs; within weeks the book was withdrawn and pulped.

27: 'Introducing Roger Hilton', *Arts* (NY), May 1957.

31: Back in Ireland Tony O'Malley had laboured for about twenty-five years as a bank official. For most of this time he had been teaching himself art (mainly in secret) until he visited St Ives for a painting holiday in 1955. He was utterly enchanted by the people, the place and the sense of creative liberation offered by such a diverse community and made a permanent move there in 1960; he very quickly became a close companion to Graham. O'Malley was an omnivorous reader of poetry (and everything else), which was much appreciated by his fellow Celt. He was also a man who enjoyed a jar accompanied by song (with his mouth organ always to hand). He set about quietly exploring the 'inscapes' of the Cornish landscape and history, that chimed with his Irish psyche, through his own unique nature based abstraction (often shaped by the flight patterns and songs of birds, all seasoned in Celtic mythology). Graham always showed a deep respect and affection for O'Malley. The two men also shared an uneasy sense of self-exile from their home turf (though for very different reasons).

32: The dedication of this poem states that Lanyon was killed in a gliding accident. This is not strictly true. On August 27 1964 Lanyon crash-landed his glider, under tricky conditions, at Dunkeswell aerodrome in Devon. Surviving the accident he was confined to bed (with a cracked vertebra) in hospital in Taunton. He died, without warning, four days later from a blood clot.

In 1985 the Tate Gallery, in London, staged a major retrospective exhibition, *St Ives 1939-1964*. The dates seem to offer a somewhat arbitrary beginning and end to the community of artists. 1939 saw the arrival of Hepworth, Nicholson and Gabo in the area, while the year of Lanyon's death was chosen to signify some significant conclusion.

41: Graham was cremated in Truro and his ashes scattered into the flux of the River Clyde. Nessie died much later on 27 May 1999 aged 89. She published her volume *Ten Poems* in 1988. In 2006 commemorative plaques were unveiled on the walls of their Madron home and Graham's birthplace in Greenock.

Picture Credits

 1: WSG outside The Sloop, photographer unknown, courtesy St Ives Archive Centre

 2: WSG ©Andrew Lanyon

 5: WSG with mirror painting, photographer unknown

 6: Photographer unknown, courtesy St Ives Archive Centre

11: Photograph by Barbara Hepworth © Bowness

19: WSG by Michael Snow 1958 © Justin Snow

20: Photographer unknown, courtesy St Ives Archive

21: WSG & Nessie by Michael Snow 1958 © Justin Snow

22: © Valerie Lowndes

23: Photographer unknown, courtesy Jonathan Riley

24/25: Courtesy Rose Hilton

28: Photographer unknown, courtesy St Ives Archive

29: © Mayotte Magnus, courtesy Rose Hilton

30: © Gail Featherston

31: © Michael Snow

32: Photographer unknown, courtesy Jonathan Riley

33: © Jane O'Malley

38: © Billy Wynter

40: © Lawrence Lawry 1978

41: © Sally Fear 1978

43: WSG by Michael Snow 1958 © Justin Snow

44: Gurnard's Head & Zennor from the Carn © David Whittaker

45: © Gail Featherston

49: © Andrew Lanyon

51: Hilton by Tony Evans © Tony Evans, courtesy Rose Hilton

54: Wynter (& son Billy) by Roger Slack © Slack Estate

56: Photographer unknown, courtesy Rose Hilton

57: Painting on card by WSG, courtesy Billy Wynter

58: Both WSG by Michael Snow 1958 © Justin Snow

60: Courtesy Frost family

61: © Sally Fear 1978

63: WSG postcard to Tony O'Malley (recuperating in hospital in St Ives from a heart Attack, 1961) courtesy Jane O'Malley

64: © Christopher Barker

Dear (Tall man mad on colour) Terry,

I got your letter about Alan. I dearly hope he is not as seriously ill as you conclude. Maybe his good greed-iness to overpower us all with talk will help his glands and organs to get over this wee bit. Your letter gave me a shock and made me realise how I would miss him not around in the great Betting Yard of the world. I know the younger Alan better. In the recent years you are nearer to him.

I understand what you mean about 'the deadly drink' and not eating. Even although some of us feel we have to take in the toxins (to maybe cushion us off ~~from~~ from the fact that our values are moving away from the normal) I would not like to hasten myself down into the burny-burny. I dreamt I dwelt in Alo Halls. "Mama Mama, the red wine burns like fire." (Translation of the first line of an aria from a Sicilian opera.) TTBB. Pour me a double.

Alco

I have written Alan from my heart and what is left of my soul. I pray to the Invisible he will get through.

I hope you are proceeding with eyes which dont see over-brown (hot) or over-blue (~~cold~~). *cold*

Love,

Letter to Terry Frost regarding Alan Lowndes (25/2/1977)

Bibliography

Books by W. S. Graham

Cage Without Grievance. Parton Press, 1942

The Seven Journeys. William MacLellan, 1944

2ND Poems. Nicholson & Watson, 1945

The White Threshold. Faber & Faber, 1949

The Nightfishing. Faber & Faber, 1955

Malcolm Mooney's Land. Faber & Faber, 1970

Implements In Their Places. Faber & Faber, 1977

Collected Poems 1942–1977. Faber & Faber, 1979

Selected Poems. Ecco Press, 1980

Uncollected Poems. Greville Press, 1990

Aimed At Nobody. Faber & Faber, 1993

Selected Poems. Faber & Faber, 1996

W. S. Graham Selected by Nessie Dunsmuir. Greville Press, 1998

The Nightfisherman: Selected Letters of W. S. Graham. Carcanet, 1999

New Collected Poems. Faber & Faber, 2004

Approaches to How They Behave. Donut Press, 2009

Studies of Graham

Duncan, R. & Davidson, J. (ed.) *The Constructed Space: A Celebration of W. S. Graham*. Jackson's Arm, 1994

Dunsmuir, N. *Ten Poems*. Greville Press, 1988

Francis, M. *Where the People Are: Language & Community in the Poetry of W. S. Graham*. Salt Publishing, 2004

Haffenden, J. 'I Would Say I Was a Happy Man: W. S. Graham Interview', Poetry Review 76, 1986

Kravitz, P. (ed.) *The Life & Works of W. S. Graham*. Edinburgh Review 75, 1987

Lopez, T. *The Poetry of W. S. Graham*. Edinburgh University Press, 1989

Pite, R. & Jones, H. (ed.) *W. S. Graham: Speaking Towards You*. Liverpool University Press, 2004

Stephens, C. *The Constructed Space*. Bradford Art Galleries & Museums, 1994

Tolley, T. (ed.) *George Barker/W. S. Graham*. Aquarius 25/26, 2002

FURTHER READING

Berlin. S. *The Coat of Many Colours*. Redcliffe, 1994

Berlin, S. *Alfred Wallis: Primitive*. Sansom & Co, 2000

Bird, M. *St Ives Artists: A Biography of Place & Time*. Lund Humphries, 2008

Bird, M. *Bryan Wynter*. Lund Humphries, 2010

Button, V. *St Ives Artists: A Companion*. Tate, 2009

Fallon, B. *Nancy Wynne-Jones*. Gandon Editions, 2002

Gooding, M. (ed.) *Painter as Critic: Patrick Heron – Selected Writings*. Tate, 2001

Lambirth, A. *Roger Hilton: The Figured Language of Thought*. Thames & Hudson, 2007

Riley, J. *Alan Lowndes*. Consruction Arts Ltd, 2010

Stephens, C. *Peter Lanyon: At the Edge of Landscape*. 21 Publishing, 2000

Whittaker, D. *Tony O'Malley: An Irish Artist in Cornwall*. Wavestone Press, 2005

STUDIO ST.IVES LTD COPYRIGHT.   GURNARD'S HEAD FROM ZENNOR HEAD